BENEDICTUS' ART DECO DESIGNS IN COLOR

With an Introduction by
Charles Rahn Fry

Dover Publications, Inc.
New York

INTRODUCTION

Edouard Benedictus was one of the outstanding artist-designers of the early twentieth century. Productive from 1900 to 1930, Benedictus witnessed, and was magnificently influenced by, the revolutionary developments in European art and design—Art Nouveau, Cubism and Constructivism among them. The following pages show Benedictus' *Variations*, the portfolio published in 1924; *Nouvelles Variations*, the portfolio published in 1926; and a selection of plates from his final portfolio, *Relais*, published posthumously in 1930. These albums are masterpieces of the style known now as Art Deco, and were produced primarily by the elaborate pochoir stencil technique.

Floral and foliate motifs abound in all three portfolios, demonstrating Benedictus' strong bonds with Art Nouveau, for which the flower and plant were central design elements. In addition to realistic shapes, there is a bounty of abstract stems, leaves, stalks and petals. Of the three albums, I find the colors in *Variations* the lushest and boldest, with the plates drenched in dark purples, reds, browns and greens highlighted by gold and silver. In *Nouvelles Variations*, the colors are muted and softer, and there is an expansion of subject matter to include animal, landscape and human forms. The plates in the *Relais* portfolio are more geometric, infused with brighter, lighter colors.

The author of an article in the French journal *Art et Décoration* in 1924 compares Benedictus' designs in *Variations* to music, with the suggestion that the 86 decorative motifs are diverse themes of a grand pictorial symphony, certain of them in the major mode and others in the minor, with the artist sometimes playing forcefully, revealing the motif brutally, and at other times modulating the theme, effacing it, making it hazy, but at all times clearly delineating the rhythm.

The design suggestions were for fabrics, textiles, upholstery and wallpaper. Patterns by Benedictus were used for the upholstery and the carpet in the Grand Salon of "Une Ambassade Française," the extraordinary French pavilion at the 1925 Exposition Internationale des Arts Décoratifs et Indus-triels Modernes. Other furnishings in the Grand Salon were by Edgar Brandt, de Corchemont, Jean Dupas, Léon Jallot, René Lalique, Raymond Subes and artists of equal stature.

Little is known of Benedictus. However, Yvanhoé Rambosson writes the following in his introduction to the *Relais* portfolio:

"Putting his encyclopedic knowledge at the service of his limitless speculative activity and curiosity, Benedictus sometimes brusquely transferred onto the practical plane with an extraordinary ease of adaptation projects that for many would have retained a visionary quality. . . . While one notes particularly his work in the applied arts, he was also a painter, writer, music lover, scientist and inventor, making remarkable forays into the most difficult areas of physics and chemistry—as he did during the war. He had an acute sense of all things, giving the impression of a medium plunging into the rhythmic secret of the world and bringing back from his journey into the beyond a sort of revelation. Accordingly he possessed a mysterious side which he retained even in his dealings with those nearest to him. Meeting him was like coming across an enchanting and swiftly flowing spring. . . .

"Where the application of art to industry was concerned, Edouard Benedictus' superiority lay in his thorough knowledge of the technology of each of the appropriate professions. Whether designing for jewelry, leather, furniture, stencils, frescoes, frames and borders, tapestries, carpets, textiles—in all these domains he made innovations, using all the potentials of machinery with the imagination of a poet. That knowledge and that understanding make a collection like this one a priceless source of concrete suggestions and further inspiration."

Far from being just collections of designs, for me the great Benedictus portfolios are an art form in themselves, monuments to their creator and to the exuberant age and brilliant society that spawned them.

CHARLES RAHN FRY

Washington, D.C.

NOTE: In the present volume, pages 1 through 20 contain (in original sequence) the entire portfolio *Variations: quatre-vingt-six motifs décoratifs en vingt planches*, originally published by the Librairie Centrale des Beaux-Arts, Paris, n.d. [1924]. Pages 21 through 40 contain (in original sequence) the entire portfolio *Nouvelles Variations: soixante-quinze motifs décoratifs en vingt planches*, originally published by Editions Albert Lévy, Librairie Centrale des Beaux-Arts, Paris, n.d. [1926]. The remaining plates are from the portfolio *Relais 1930: quinze planches donnant quarante-deux motifs décoratifs*, Editions Vincent, Fréal et Cie, Paris, n.d. [1930]; pages 41 through 46 of the present volume contain the *Relais* plates originally numbered 1, 4, 5, 6, 8 and 9, respectively; original plate 14 appears on the inside front cover of this volume, original plate 12 on the inside back cover. Four other plates from *Relais* appear in the Dover volume *Art Deco Designs in Color*, edited by Charles Rahn Fry (1975).

Published in Canada by General Publishing Company, Ltd., 30 Lesmill Road, Don Mills, Toronto, Ontario.

Published in the United Kingdom by Constable and Company, Ltd., 10 Orange Street, London WC2H 7EG.

Benedictus' Art Deco Designs in Color, first published by Dover Publications, Inc., in 1980, contains plates from the portfolios listed in the Introduction and Note above. All the plates are from the collection of Charles Rahn Fry.

International Standard Book Number: 0-486-23971-3
Library of Congress Catalog Card Number: 79-57041

Manufactured in the United States of America
Dover Publications, Inc.
180 Varick Street
New York, N.Y. 10014

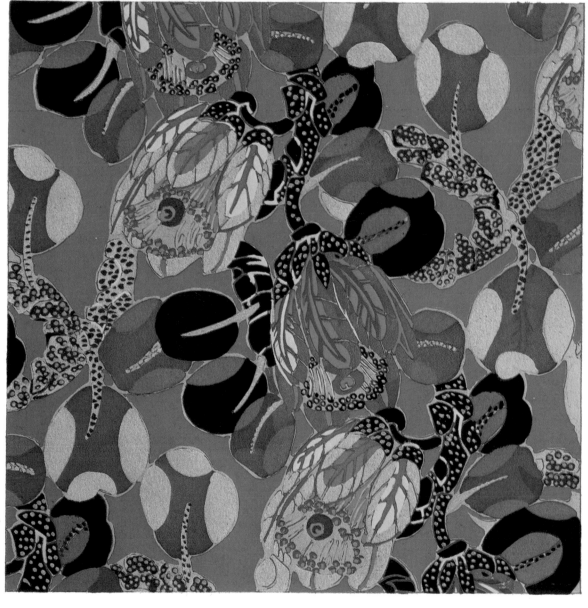

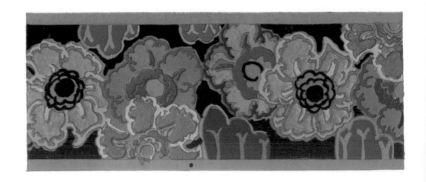

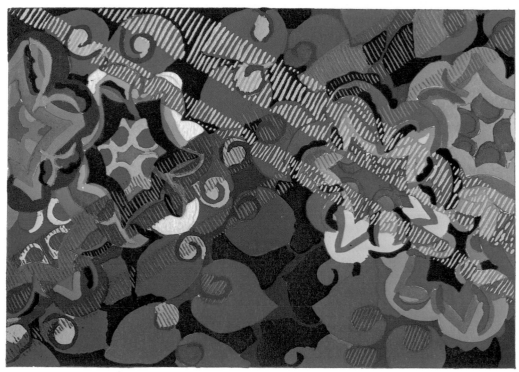

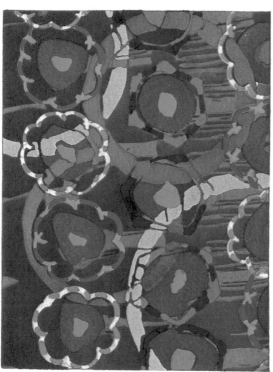

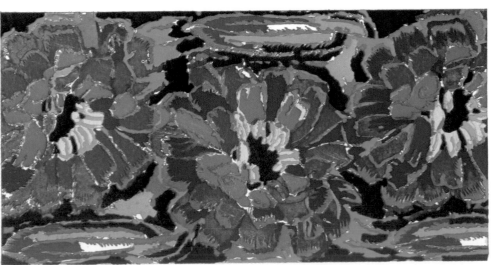

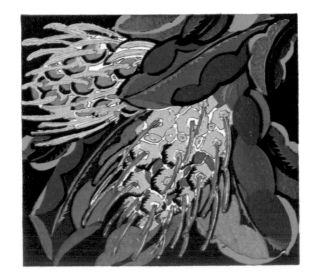

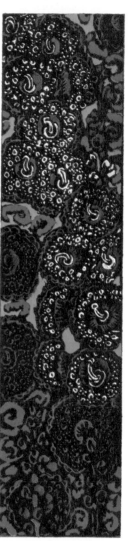

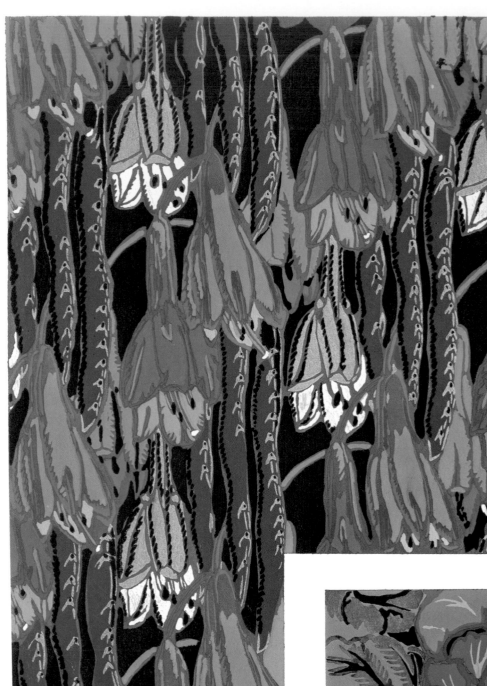

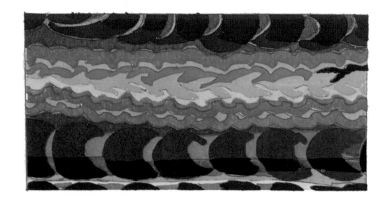

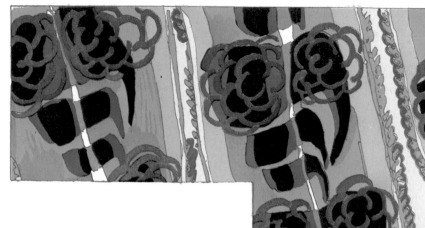

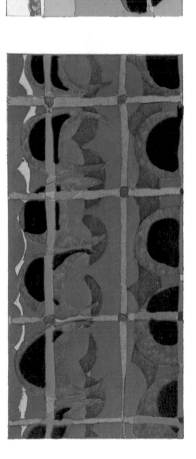

14

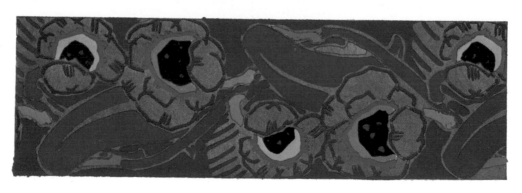

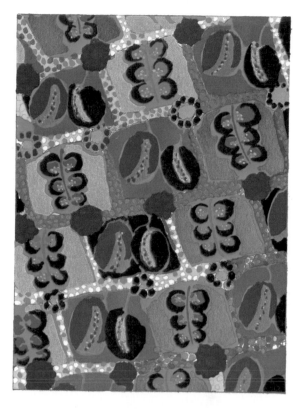

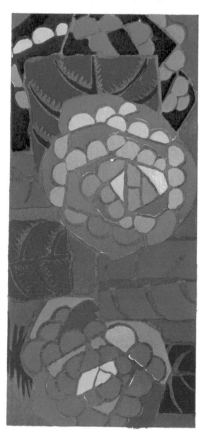

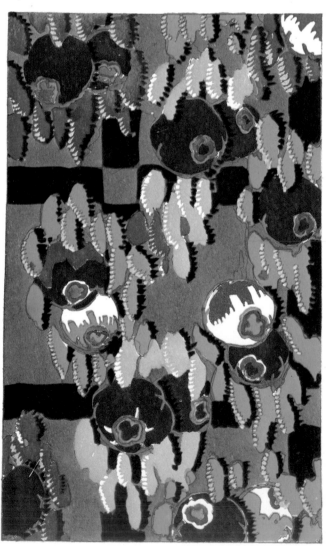

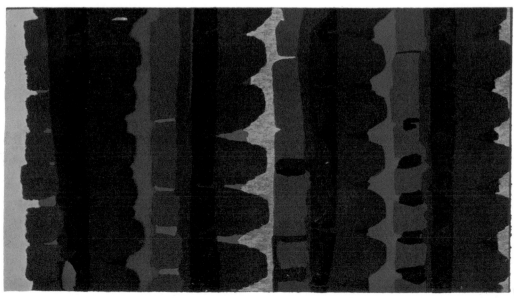

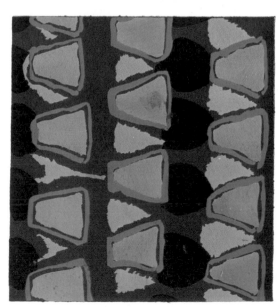

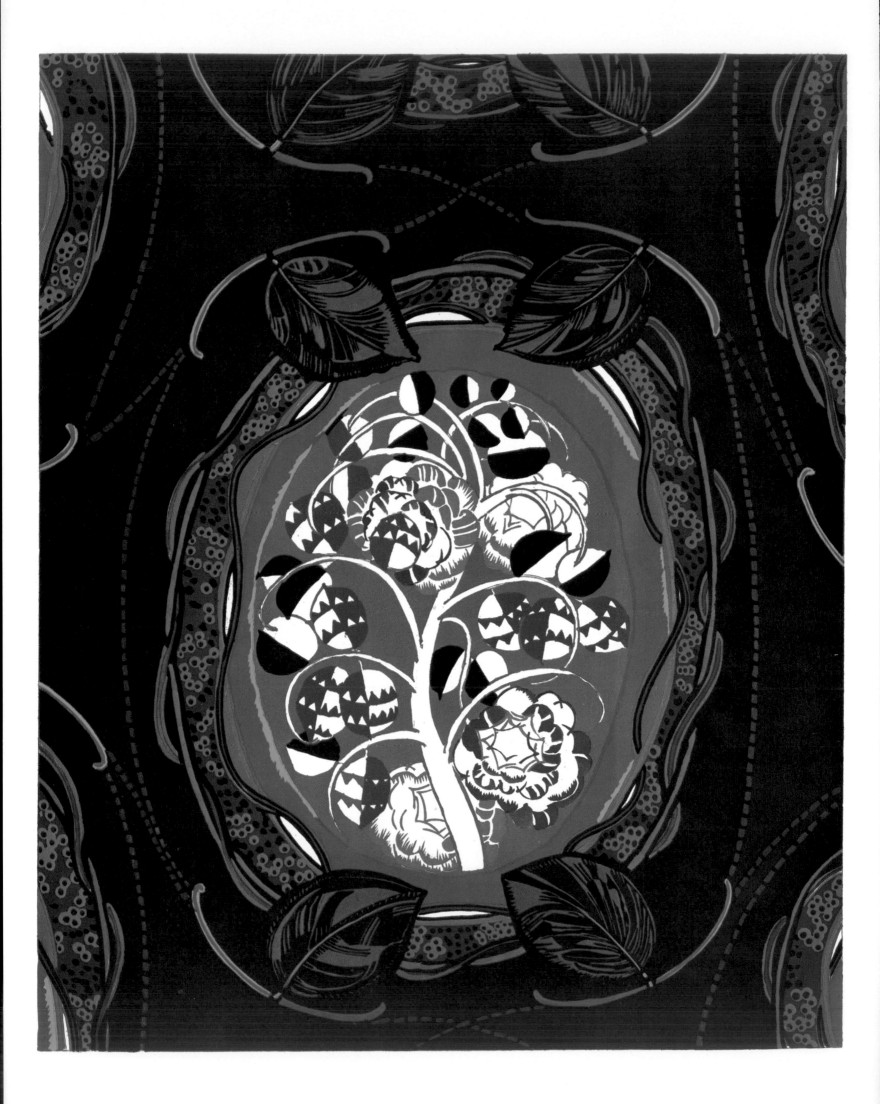

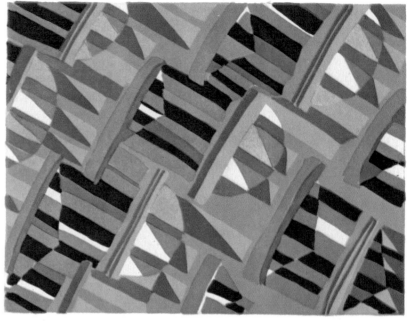

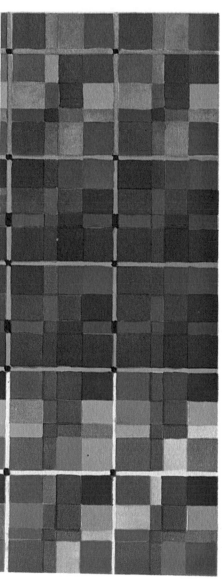

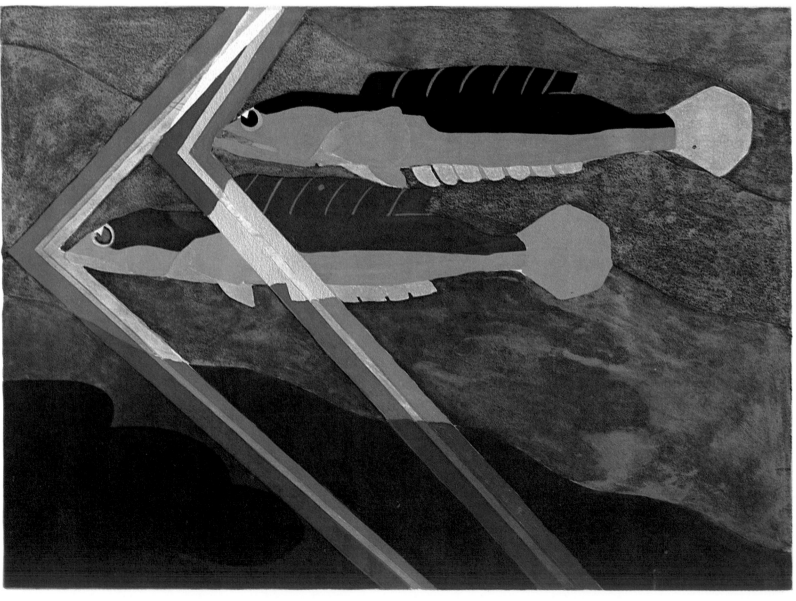

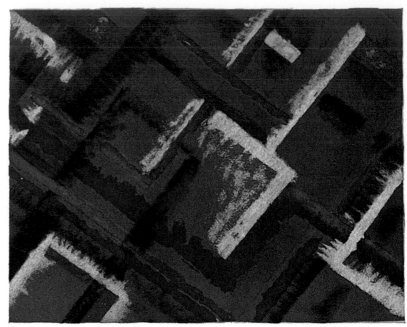

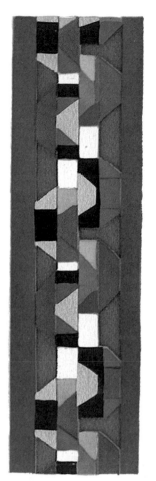

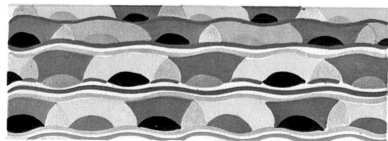

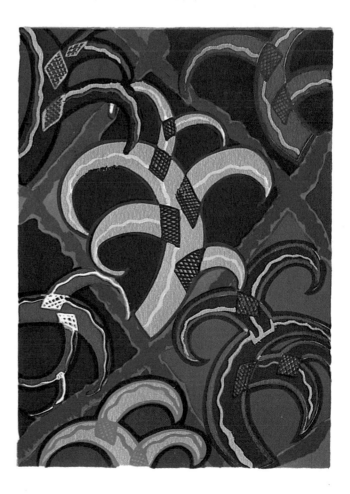

33

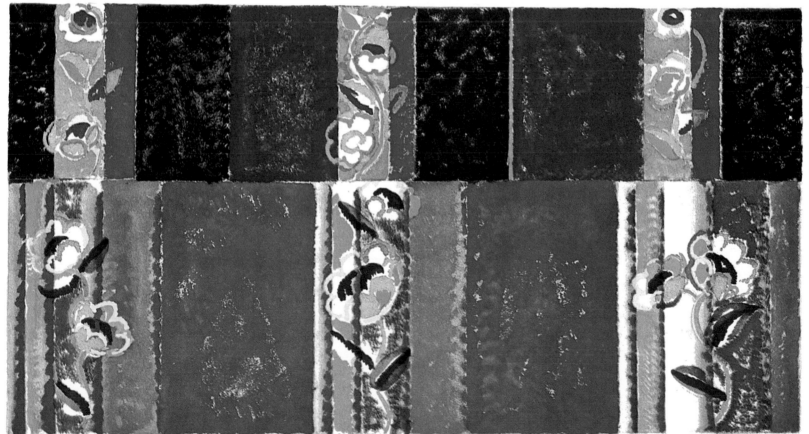

38

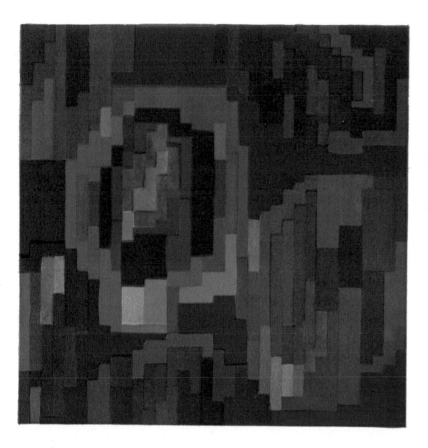

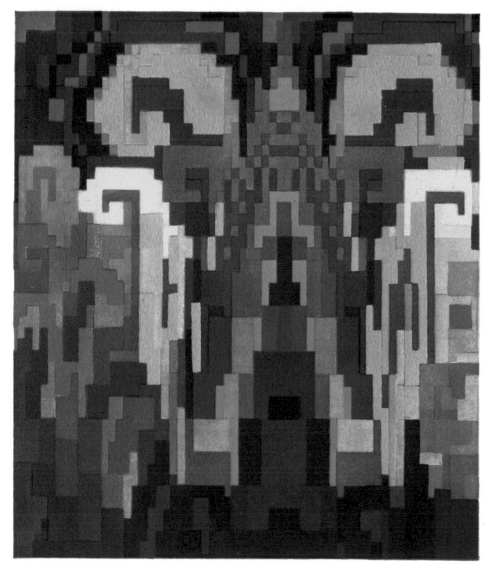